WHO ARE YOU WITHOUT THAT?

A Woman's Journey from Performance and Approval to Healing, Identity, Authenticity, and Wholeness

Tacondra L. Brown

For the woman who has been performing her whole life — and the one underneath the image who has been waiting to be found.

"Before I formed you in the womb I knew you."
- Jeremiah 1:5

Contents

INTRODUCTION

*What if the image you've been living your entire life…
isn't really you?*

Not the image you built for a platform. Not the one you curated for social media. Not the one you perfected for the boardroom, the family reunions and social events, or even the mirror you avoid on the hard days. Not the image shaped by the women who raised you, the men who stayed or left, the tags and titles you earned, or the roles you were assigned including the ones before you were old enough to know what you wanted. What if all of it…the whole carefully constructed, exhaustively maintained, image of who you think you are supposed to be — was built on a foundation that was never yours? A foundation that isn't true to who you are? And what if the woman you were born to be, before the world got its hands on you and started telling you who to be, has been standing underneath all of it this whole time?

Patiently waiting to arise.

That's what this book is about. It's about looking beyond the image you were given and the one you built and shedding the performed identity that you've likely benefited from but has been wearing you out for years. It's about healing the distorted, wound-shaped reflections you have been mistaking for the truth about who you are. And to reclaim the woman you were born to be, and the woman God already knew.

She existed before the performance started. Before the labels multiplied. Before the approval-seeking became survival and the survival became a lifestyle and the lifestyle became so familiar you stopped questioning whether it was even yours.

She existed before it all.

And she is exactly who we are going to find in these pages. I know because I had to find her myself. I'm still discovering more about her along my journey.

I remember growing up as a little girl playing softball. I wasn't a huge fan of the game itself…I didn't like getting dirty. But I admired softball because I watched my dad, my mom, my aunts and uncles play. So, it only made sense that my dad's twin daughters would play too. Of course, I'm one of those twins.

I didn't realize it at the time, but I wasn't playing softball because I loved it. I was playing because I wanted my dad to be proud. I wanted his approval. I wanted to be like everyone else I admired and to feel accepted. I wanted my family to see me as part of something bigger than myself.

And so, I performed. I put on my cleats, stepped up to the plate, and tried my hardest to be what I thought I was supposed to be. Except, it wasn't who I really was.

I was a lover of music. Art. Singing. Piano.

That small childhood moment was only the beginning. From the time we are little girls, we learn something that goes far deeper than preference. We learn that acceptance comes with performance. Gold stars on our schoolwork teach us that effort is only valuable when it's rewarded. Applause for our talents tells us that worth is measured by how well we entertain. The smiles of approval when we conform remind us that belonging often comes at the cost of authenticity.

And without realizing it, we grow up to become women who have quietly shaped our entire lives around the expectations of others.

The Performance Continues

The same girl who longed for approval on the softball field grows into the woman who seeks validation in the workplace, in relationships, on social media platforms, and even in her faith. And the need to be seen, significant, supported, accepted, and valued doesn't simply disappear. *It evolves.*

Maybe you can relate? In your career endeavors, you become the one who stays late, takes on extra projects, and pushes yourself past exhaustion to be seen. Not always because you want to, but because you are afraid of being seen as incapable or replaceable. You measure your success not by how fulfilled you feel, but by how much recognition you receive. The promotion, the title, the salary…all of it becomes proof that you are enough. But when you pause long enough to breathe, you can't help but wonder at times: *Do I even love this?*

In your relationships, you mold yourself into who you believe others want or need you to be. You shapeshift to fit in, you downplay your needs, silence your opinions, and wear masks of perfection, fearing that if you are fully honest, seen, messy, flawed and human, you will no longer be liked or loved. And deep down, resentment is growing. Because you have given so much of yourself away that there is hardly anything left.

If you're a believer, you may understand how even in our faith journey we learn to perform. Maybe you're the woman who attends church every Sunday, like I did, and you aren't yet mature in your walk with Christ. You might not notice it, but subconsciously you're checking the right boxes to fit in with others and to be in right standing with God. You quote the right scriptures, say the right words, perform the right responsibilities, join the right ministries looking to belong and live as if your worthiness is something to be earned, rather than received because you are already loved. Instead of resting in God's love for just being, you exhaust yourself trying to prove you deserve it from leaders and others. Sometimes at the expense of your family, finances, and more.

Am I talking to you?

The tragedy of performance is that it is never satisfied. External validation is a hunger that cannot be filled. It only grows.

What happens when the roles you played so well are stripped away through loss, failure, or transition? When you are no longer the successful one, the pretty one, the perfect wife, the best mom, the strong friend, the faithful woman of God, or the one who has it all together? Who are you when there is nothing left to perform for?

That is where the real journey begins. Not in striving, but in stripping away. Not in becoming someone new, but in rediscovering who you were before the world, people, or even trauma told you who to be. These are the questions I have asked myself. It's the journey I'm still navigating with grace. It wasn't until I found myself sitting at a lagoon in Belize — having dropped everything, left everything, and stripped away every role and title I had been hiding behind — that I finally understood what had been happening my entire life.

I had been living from a formed identity. One built from the outside in. Constructed from roles, titles, wounds, survival, performance and borrowed pieces of another woman's essence. Maintained by exhaustion and held together by the fear of who I would be if I stopped. And underneath all of it was something else entirely.

My born identity.

The woman God knew before I was ever formed.

In the pages ahead we are going to do three things together, for the most part:

1. Unravel, honestly and without shame, the identity that was formed around you without your full permission.

2. Reclaim the born identity that has been buried underneath it.

3. Talk about what it looks like to integrate the information being discussed and how to actually live from that place — rooted, real, and radiant in a way no performance could ever produce.

Now, before you begin this journey, I want to tell you something: I haven't fully arrived yet. And you won't either by the time you finish reading this book. But the words penned in these pages are layered with ah-ha moments, action steps and pearls to help you along your journey.

It is part story, part mirror, part map. Some chapters will land directly in the center of where you are right now. Others may speak to a season you have already walked through and reading them will feel like finally getting the language for something you navigated but never fully understood. Some words may speak to a season that is still ahead of you, quietly preparing you for what is coming before you even know it is on its way.

Not every chapter will be your chapter. And that is okay too.

I like to move between topics the way life moves. Not always in a straight line, not always in the order we would choose, but always with intention and purpose. So, if you find yourself reading a section and thinking *this does not apply to me or is not where I am right now*, keep going anyway. Chew the meat, spit out the bones, and fill in the gaps. There is something in these pages for every version of you. The woman you were. The woman you are. And the woman you are still becoming.

Read it like a journey. Read it like a map. Not a map with a single route, but the kind that shows you where you are, marks where you have been, and points toward where you are going. The kind that reminds you that even when you feel lost, you are never without direction. Read it like a conversation. Read it like a friend who has been where you are, sat down across from you, ordered two cups of coffee, and decided to tell you the truth. Whole truth. Nothing but the truth.

I'm that friend, okay!

Your story may not look like mine. But the destination is the same: to Reclaim, Rebuild, and Radiate your authentic and whole self.

I don't know about you, but I'm done performing.

Are you ready?

PART ONE

THE UNRAVELING

When Your Identity Has Been Shaken

CHAPTER ONE

WHO AM I WITHOUT THAT?

The roles you play are not the woman you are. They are the costume. Underneath is someone far more original.

There is a question most high-achieving women never let themselves ask out loud. Not because they don't feel it, but because feeling it is kinda scary. Saying it out loud makes it real.

> *Who am I without that?*

Without the role. Without the title. Without the degrees. Without the certifications, licenses, and the salary. Without the relationship. Without the things that have quietly been holding your sense of self together for longer than you probably realize.

If that question just landed somewhere in your body, this chapter is for you.

The Labels You Inherited

From the moment you arrived in this world, someone was already deciding who you were. Daughter. Sister. The smart one. The pretty one. The responsible one. The oldest child. The middle child. The baby. Before you were old enough to have an opinion about who you'd like to be, you had already been assigned a role.

And, of course, you accepted the assignment. Because what else do we do when we're five years old and the people we love most are smiling at us for being exactly what they named us, right?

So, you grew into the tiles, roles, and labels. You learned to perform them well. And without realizing it, you learned the most dangerous lesson of your young life: who you are is what you do, and what you do determines whether you are loved. We don't often realize it, but we carry this lesson into adolescence. Into adulthood. Into our career choices, the bedroom, the church pews, the family dinner table, the communities we live in. And the labels continued to multiply.

> *Wife. Mother. Businesswoman. CEO. Mentor. Caregiver. The strong friend. The one who holds it all together.*

Each role carries its own weight. Its own unspoken rules about how much you are supposed to give, and how little you are supposed to need. For years, you pour yourself into these identities. And as long as all of it stayed in place, you could almost convince yourself you knew who you were.

> *Almost.*

Now don't get me wrong. Roles and relationships are not the enemy. Being a mother, a wife, a leader, a friend — those are beautiful things. The problem is not that we have roles.

The problem is when the role becomes you.

Here's what you eventually realize along your journey: roles are not permanent. Relationships change. Titles are taken. Children grow up. Jobs end. Marriages fracture. Things happen in life that shake you. And when the thing that was holding your identity together gets disrupted or disappears, you are left standing with the broken pieces of a life that used to make sense, asking: *Who am I without all of that?*

Maybe you are the high-achieving career woman who lost her job and suddenly questioned your worth because your identity was built on what you do and your income. Somewhere along the way, your productivity became your identity. Maybe you are the devoted wife or a woman going through a divorce and wonder if you still belong anywhere. You've shaped yourself so much around being someone's wife that you don't even know who you are or even who you were before that. Hello, *I can relate to that one!*

Maybe you are the mother whose child grew up and moved away, and now you feel a quiet emptiness where your sense of purpose used to be.

HOLD PLEASE.

Hang out with me and take a moment to dive deeper right here, right now, because nobody prepares a mother for this one. *I sure wasn't ready.* You know, the world tends to frame empty nesting as one specific story. It can look like the graduation party. The college send-off. The teary goodbye in a dorm room doorway with a car full of bedding and a mini fridge. But empty nest does not always arrive wrapped up in celebration. Sometimes a child leaves because they are ready and thriving and building a life of their own and that is beautiful. Sometimes a child leaves because of conflict, because of choices, because of a falling out that nobody saw coming and nobody quite knows how to fix.

Sometimes they leave for a relationship. Sometimes for a lifestyle. Sometimes they simply drift until one day you look up and realize the daily presence of them is just gone. Every single departure can leave you standing in the same silence asking the same question.

Who am I without them?

Regardless of how it arrives or what causes it, empty nest syndrome is real and it's about the moment you realize that a significant portion of your daily identity, your sense of purpose, your reason for structuring your time the way you structured it, was built around the hands-on, *they-need-me* version of motherhood. And suddenly, that version is over. Motherhood itself does not end. But that season of it does. And very rarely does anyone warn you it is coming until it has already arrived.

Maybe your children leaving is or will be joyful. Maybe it's been or will be painful. Maybe it's complicated in ways that do not fit neatly into either category. But either way, pride and grief can live in the same breath. And you can feel both so deeply while not knowing which one is louder.

And if you only have one child, *whew*, it hits way different because there is no redirecting of your love. There is no other child to fold yourself into. There is just the space where they used to be. And you standing in it. Trying to figure out who you are now. By the way, if that *is* you, I highly recommend you get a pet, if you haven't already.

I remember when my daughter left home for the first time. I thought something was wrong with me. Random bursts of emotions, tears, depression, whatever! You name it, I probably had it. Suddenly there was no one outside of my husband to cook for. No one to awake after sleeping in all morning. No one to pour into in the daily, ordinary, unglamorous ways that motherhood shows up. No one to manage. And if I am being honest, that loss of control, that loss of being needed in that specific way, shook something in me I was not expecting.

Here is what I did not realize until it happened: I had quietly built a significant portion of my identity around being her mother. The morning routines. The school lunch dates. The pickups. The after-school activities. The dinners. The birthday parties. The conversations that happened in the car when she didn't even know what she was listening to. All of it was not just mothering, it was me. It was how I knew who I was every single day. And when that season ended abruptly, I found myself grieving, not just her absence, but the version of myself that only existed in relation to her presence. There is more to this story, which I'll get into later. But I share this transparently, as a teen mom who is now in her forties at the time of writing this book, to say that these moments are not small losses. And they are not failures as a mom. They are the inevitable consequence of building a home inside something that was never designed to be permanent.

Your children are never meant to be the foundation. They are meant to be the fruit. And here is what I want to say to the mother who is not quite there yet — the one whose children are still young, still home, still needing you in all the ways that feel like your whole purpose right now:

You will be here before you know it.

Not to frighten you. But to lovingly invite you to begin preparing your heart now so that when the time and silence does come, you are not meeting yourself as a stranger.

Preparing Your Heart Before the Nest Empties

If your children are still home and you aren't already doing these things, here are a few things I wish my mother or someone else would have told me. Do not wait until they leave to start doing this work:

1. **Start reconnecting with who you were before you became mom.** Pull out the things you set down when motherhood began. The hobby you gave up. The dream you deferred. The part of you that existed before the title. Begin investing in her again in small, imperfect ways. Take a class. Pick up the instrument. Start writing. Go somewhere alone just because you want to. She needs tending now so she is not a stranger when you need her later.

2. **Build an identity that exists alongside your role as mother, not inside of it.** This does not mean you love your children less. It means you are more than what you do for them. Begin intentionally cultivating friendships, passions, purpose, and community that belong entirely to you. These become your anchors when the role shifts.

3. **Have the honest conversation with yourself about what motherhood has been giving you.** Has it been giving you

purpose? Identity? Distraction from your own unhealed places? A reason to pour outward so you do not have to look inward? There is no judgment in the answer. But the more honest you are now, the less blindsided you will be later.

4. **Begin transferring your sense of purpose from what you do to who you are.** Purpose rooted in a role will always be fragile because roles change. Purpose rooted in identity endures. Ask yourself: outside of being someone's mother, what do I believe I am here to do? What do I carry that the world needs? Begin building toward that answer now.

5. **Practice letting go in small ways while they are still home.** From the moment you give birth to your children, you're being prepared to let them go even as they learn to take steps away from you as a child. Your heart knows this, but it won't connect with what you already know when the time arrives for them to leave the nest. So, let them make more decisions while they are young. Let them fail in low-stakes situations. Let them need you less in the small daily things. This is not detachment, it is preparation. For them and for you. You are practicing the healthy release that will be required of you fully when they leave. The more you practice it now, the more natural it becomes.

6. **Get into community with women who are ahead of you in this season.** Find the mothers whose children have already left. The ones who have navigated the silence and found themselves on the other side of it. Let them mentor you into this transition. Ask them what they wish they had done differently. Their hindsight is your gift.

There is beauty and purpose in being a mom. But always remember, you are a woman beyond the mothering. You were someone before they arrived, and you are someone after they leave. And that woman who exists outside of the role deserves just as much of your attention, your investment, and your love as the children you pour everything into.

This matters. Let's keep going.

The Exhaustion Nobody Talks About

If you've ever felt tired, not just physically tired, but tired in your soul…there is a reason. And it is not because you're weak. It is not due to a lack of gratitude. It is not even a sign that something is wrong with you. It is likely due to the exhaustion of performing for approval. Because that is most likely what you have been doing.

Showing up in roles you were assigned or chose, giving everything you must to maintain an image of who you are supposed to be. And somewhere in the middle of all of it, quietly losing touch with who you are. *Ask me how I know!*

Most high-achieving women struggle with people-pleasing. We become the fixers. The ones who say yes when every part of us is screaming no. We often learn to wear masks of perfection because we are terrified that if we are fully seen as we are, we will no longer be liked, loved or respected.

And deep down, resentment grows. Yeah, it's there. Whether you realize it or not. Not because you are ungrateful. But because you have given so much of yourself away for so long that there is hardly anything left. And you start to grieve a version of yourself you can barely remember. Or never had the chance to know.

I know that feeling. I lived inside it for years.

The scary thing about losing yourself is that it doesn't happen all at once.

It starts small. You agree with something you don't believe because disagreeing feels like too much. You let go of a dream because someone you love doesn't understand it or you don't have the support to build it. You stop wearing the colors you love because someone made a comment once. You stop saying the thing that's true because the room doesn't seem ready for it.

You adapt. You adjust. You shrink.

But what you're really doing is trading pieces of yourself for acceptance. One compromise at a time.

Until the woman looking back at you in the mirror is a curated version: Polished. Easy digestible. Acceptable. And she eventually becomes exhausted because it takes a lot of energy to be someone you are not. Every single day.

Signs You've Been Living for Validation

Before you can reclaim *who* you are, you must be honest about where you've been. Who you've been. Not with shame, but with the kind of honesty that is really an act of love toward yourself. You feel lost when you're not needed. When there is nothing to do, no one to fix, no role to fill — you feel anxious or empty. Stillness doesn't always feel like rest. It can feel like failure. Like you aren't being productive.

Perhaps, your self-worth fluctuates with other people's opinions? One piece of criticism can easily undo a hundred compliments. Maybe you are only as confident as your last review? Do you even know what you *really* want in life? Ask yourself right now: What do

I want? Not what needs to get done. Not what would make those kids, that husband, or anyone else happy. What do *you* want?

If the answer doesn't come quickly, that is information worth sitting with.

You've probably shrunk yourself more than your ideal share of times to make others comfortable. You've made yourself smaller in your opinions and your presence just because someone in your life couldn't handle the full version of you. And somewhere along the way, you started to believe that the smaller version was the real you.

If any of those landed — and I suspect more than one did — you are not alone. You are simply a woman who was never taught to build her identity from the inside out. And that is exactly what we are about to do.

FRAMEWORK: THE IDENTITY AUDIT

This exercise helps you identify which parts of your identity are truly yours — and which were assigned, borrowed, or built for survival. Set aside 20-30 minutes, a journal, and a quiet space.

Step 1: List Your Labels:

Write down every role, title, and label that currently defines you. Include everything — mother, wife, boss, caregiver, the strong friend, the smart one. Don't filter. Just list.

Step 2: Ask the Hard Question:

For each label, ask: Did I choose this, or was it given to me? Does this role energize me or deplete me? Would I still choose it if there were no external pressure?

Step 3: Identify the Borrowed Pieces:

Which parts of who you are did you model from someone else? A parent, a mentor, a woman you admired? Circle anything that doesn't feel originally yours.

Step 4: Find the Constant:

Now ask: What has been true about me since I was a little girl — before the world started making requests? What do I return to when everything else falls away? *That is your born identity speaking.*

Step 5: Name What Stays:

Of everything on your list, what do you choose to keep? What belongs to the real you? What are you ready to lay down? Write it out. This is your first act of reclamation.

You don't have to complete this in one sitting. Return to it as many times as you need. The goal is not perfection, it is honest inventory.

The Question Underneath the Question

Who am I without that?

I want to offer you a reframe. Because I know how frightening that question feels. But I also know this: that question is not an ending. It is an invitation. It is your soul finally asking, after years of performing, to come home.

The woman you are without the title, without the role, without the validation? She has been there all along. Waiting for you to stop being so busy performing that you could finally sit still long enough to hear her. She is who God made you to be. Before anyone had an opinion about it. And she is not lost.

She is buried. Underneath the years of performance, the layers of adaptation, the weight of everyone else's expectations.

Buried is not gone. And this — right here — is where the unraveling begins.

REFLECT

What roles or titles have you built your identity around and what would you feel without them?

____

____

____

____

When is the last time you did something purely because it was true to who you are?

____

____

____

____

What version of yourself have you quietly let go of to be more acceptable to others?

____

____

____

____

If no one was watching and no one would have an opinion, who would you be?

CHAPTER TWO

WHEN CONFIDENCE IS CRUSHED

Rock bottom has a gift buried inside it and that gift is this: there is nothing left to protect. No image to uphold. No performance to maintain.

There is a kind of breaking that doesn't announce itself.

It doesn't arrive with one clean, devastating blow that you can point to and say — that's the moment. It comes in waves. One after another. And just when you think you've found your footing, another one hits. Until one day you realize you're not standing anymore. You're just trying not to go under.

If you know that feeling, this chapter is yours.

Before the Breaking

Before December 2021, I had a vision. I was building something — a personal brand rooted in healing and transformation. Writing books, hosting events, showing up for women behind the scenes who were walking the same roads I had walked. It wasn't perfect. It wasn't finished. But it was mine. And it was moving.

I had some momentum. I had authority. I had a sense of purpose that got me out of bed in the morning. I didn't know it then, but I was about to learn something that no vision board prepares you for.

Life doesn't ask permission before it dismantles everything you've built.

December 2021

The call came, and everything stopped.

My daddy had a massive stroke.

If you've ever watched someone you love suddenly become fragile, different…it breaks something inside you.

I did what any loving daughter would do.

I dropped everything.

The brand. The books. The future events. The vision. The foundation I had spent years building from scratch. All of it. I set it down like it weighed nothing, because in that moment, it did.

My dad needed me.

I became a caregiver, alongside my mom and my sisters at the time. I showed up the way a daughter shows up when the people who raised them need them most. Without thinking twice, without counting the cost, without asking whether I could afford to. Because that is what love does. It goes. And showing up for him was right.

I want to say that clearly, before I say anything else. I do not regret it. I would do it again. But nobody, not one person, could have prepared me for what it would cost me. I became fragile emotionally in a way I had never experienced before. I am a strong woman. I have always been a strong woman, thanks to being a military wife. Strength was my identity, my survival mechanism. But caregiving — the kind that is relentless and without a finish line, the kind where you pour and pour and pour and the pouring never seems to be enough — it broke through every wall of strength I ever had.

I cried in my car. I cried in the shower. I cried in the quiet moments between doing all the things that needed to be done, when no one was watching and I finally had permission to fall apart for sixty seconds before pulling myself back together and going back to the new normal way of living.

We talk about grief like it only belongs to loss. Like it only shows up at funerals when someone is gone. But there is another kind of grief that nobody prepares you for. The kind that sits at the dinner table with you. The kind that holds your hand in the waiting rooms. The kind that looks back at you with familiar eyes from a face that is still here, still breathing, still present, but somehow different from the person you have always known.

That is its own language of pain.

Grieving someone who has passed is devastating. But there is a particular kind of ache that comes with grieving someone who is still alive. Still yours. But changed in ways you cannot reverse and cannot fully accept and cannot stop loving them through. Nobody tells you about that grief. Nobody gives you a casserole for it. Nobody sends flowers. Nobody knows quite what to say because the person is still here…and so the world keeps moving like every-thing is fine.

But you know it is not fine. And you grieve anyway. Privately.

I began to drift spiritually. And that frightened me more than anything else. There had always been something in me that could find God in worship, in the Word, in prayer, in a quiet moment of surrender. But that season stripped even that away. I could no longer utter a prayer. The words would not come. Not because I stopped believing, but because I was so emptied out that even the language of faith felt like a performance and something I no longer had access to. I would open my Bible and sit there staring at words that used to move me, waiting for something to land and nothing would. The silence was deafening. The fight of faith became frustrating and lonelier than I know how to describe.

Financially, things began to unravel. I went from building a platform to being buried under the weight of someone else's survival.

Physically exhausted. Mentally depleted.

But I kept going. Because that's what you do when you're the strong one, right?

August 2022

I thought I had seen my lowest point. I hadn't.

About eight months after my dad's stroke, my only child — my daughter — came to me with something I wasn't prepared for. She was in a relationship with a girl. Remember I talked about emp-ty-nester syndrome earlier in the book? Yeah, it all ties together from this moment of my journey.

I'm going to be honest with you the way I hope this book teaches you to be honest with yourself: that knocked me down. Hard. Not because I stopped loving her. I never stopped, not for a single second. But because everything about her choice collided with everything I had built my faith around. And when your faith and your love for your child feel like they're standing on opposite sides of a line, that is a different kind of broken. She is my only child. The one I poured into and prayed over. And in one conversation, I found myself standing in a place I had no map for. Grieving something I couldn't fully name. Wrestling with a God I thought I understood.

What do you do when the thing you believe and the person you love most are asking you to choose?

I didn't have an answer then. I still don't have a complete answer now. But what I did end up doing at that time was what I had always done. I buried it. And went back to work.

Rock Bottom Has a Zip Code

My husband and I went back to work full time together. Not because we wanted to, but because we had to. My dad needed care. Our family needed more stability. So, we showed up every day to jobs that had nothing to do with who we were, and we did what needed to be done.

After nine months, I burnt out.

Not the kind of burnout where you take a long weekend and feel better. The kind where your body just stops. Refuses. The kind where you look up one day and something inside you says, I cannot do this anymore.

I walked away from that job. So did my husband. And then we made a decision that probably looked like we were either living our best lives or losing our minds from the outside.

We left. Left the job. Left our daughter. Left my dad and family. Left Texas. Left the United States entirely. We moved to Belize.

The Backyard of Everything

There is something about getting far enough away from your life that you can finally see it clearly. In Belize, there was a lagoon that led into the ocean behind our house. I sat there daily. Not performing for anyone. Not caregiving, not working, not holding anything together. Just sitting with the water. With the silence. With myself.

And that is where the unraveling began. Not the kind of unraveling that destroys, the kind that reveals. Sitting at that lagoon, I began to see something I had never been able to see from inside my life: I had been living in survival mode. Not for a season — for most of my life. Surviving. Self-sacrificing. Playing the savior. Pouring myself out for everyone around me and calling it strength, calling it love, calling it purpose.

And it was all rooted in something. A formed identity. Built from the outside in — from what I survived, what I performed, what I sacrificed, what I was told I was or who I thought I had to be.

At that lagoon in Belize, I began to understand the difference between the woman I had formed myself to be and the woman God had born me to be.

They were not the same woman. And knowing the difference was the beginning of everything.

What Crushing Your Confidence Actually Looks Like

Maybe your breaking point wasn't a stroke or a move to another country. Maybe it will be quieter. But perhaps you recognize the feeling. You stop trusting yourself, not just your decisions, but your instincts. The inner voice that used to speak clearly has gone silent because you've overridden it so many times it stopped trying.

You shrink from visibility. The thing you used to build or create starts to feel too risky. What if you fail again? So, you stay small. Stay quiet. Stay safe. You grieve a version of yourself you can't get back. The woman you were before the loss, before the thing that changed everything. You're not sure she's coming back.

You keep moving, but the light is gone. You function. You show up. But something vital is missing. You are going through the motions of a life that used to feel like yours. If you're nodding in agreement, please hear this: that is not the end of your story. That is the ground being cleared for something real to be built.

FRAMEWORK: MAPPING YOUR BREAKING POINTS

Understanding the seasons that broke you is essential to rebuilding. This exercise helps you trace the origin of your confidence wounds so you can stop carrying them as permanent truth.

Step 1: Name the Season:

Write down the season, event, or period in your life where your confidence was most deeply shaken. Be specific. Name the year, the circumstance, what you lost.

Step 2: Identify the Belief It Created:

What story did that breaking point create about you? Finish this sentence honestly: After that happened, I began to believe I was ________________. (Not enough. Unlovable. Cursed. Behind. Too much. Not capable.)

Step 3: Trace the Behavior:

How has that belief shaped your behavior since? Did you over-achieve, withdraw, perform harder, stop trying? Can you trace decisions you've made from that wound?

Step 4: Separate the Event from the Meaning:

The event happened. But the meaning you gave it — that is a story, not a fact. Ask: Is this belief actually true? What evidence exists that it isn't?

Step 5: Find the Gift:

This is the hard one. What did the breaking give you that you couldn't have received any other way? Strength, clarity, compassion, direction? Even painful seasons carry gifts. Name one.

You may need to return to this framework with a therapist or trusted mentor for deeper breaking points. This exercise is a beginning — not a substitute for professional support when needed.

What the Breaking Is Really For

The breaking was not punishment. It was not abandonment. It was not proof that God had looked away.

The breaking was an invitation. An invitation to stop building on a foundation that was never going to hold. To stop performing a version of strength that was actually just survival wearing a costume.

Rock bottom has a gift buried inside it and that gift is this: there is nothing left to protect. No image to uphold. No performance to maintain. No more pretending.

And in that terrifying, humbling, holy nakedness — you finally get to meet yourself. Not the formed version. Not the survival version. The original one. The one who was here before all of this.

She is still in there. I promise you she is.

And the next chapter is about finding her.

> *"He heals the brokenhearted and binds up their wounds."*
> *— Psalm 147:3*

REFLECT

What has been your breaking point, the moment or season that shook your identity to its core?

____

____

____

____

In what ways have you been living in survival mode and calling it strength?

____

____

____

____

What have you been sacrificing of yourself in the name of love or duty?

____

____

____

____

What did the breaking take from you and what, if anything, did it quietly give you?

CHAPTER THREE

HEALING THE BROKEN MIRROR

You are not barren. You are bearing fruit — in ways you may not be able to see yet. But they are real. They are growing. And they are rooted in something no setback could ever reach.

You have seen the breaking. You have traced the unraveling through the seasons that dismantled everything you built, the roles, the titles, the version of yourself you held together with sheer will and exhausting performance.

But before anything can be reclaimed, something else has to happen first. Something more internal than the collapse itself.

Because here is what rock-bottom reveals, if you are willing to look: it is not just the roles that crumbled. It is the stories underneath the roles. The beliefs you built in the wreckage of every loss, every disappointment, every silence from God you interpreted as absence. The narratives you adopted about yourself that have been shaping every decision, every relationship, every quiet moment of self-assessment since.

Before the healing. Before the reclaiming. Before any of the work in Part Two of this book becomes possible, the broken mirror must be found.

Not the surface stuff. Not the *I need to work on my confidence* stuff. I mean the deep narrative. The wounds that have been shaping your so-called "wisdom." The story running underneath everything that you rarely say out loud because saying it out loud would make it too real.

The one that says: I'm barren. God is disappointed in me.

That was the story I kept telling myself. Maybe yours sounds like: I must prove myself to be seen as significant. Or I always lose what matters most. Or I must be cursed because this keeps happening to me. Or the quietest, most devastating one of all…I am not enough. I am not loved.

That is the broken mirror. And until it is healed, everything you see — yourself, your future, your relationships with others and even with God — will be distorted by it.

Where the Lie Began

For me, the broken mirror had a specific origin. It didn't start with my dad's stroke or my daughter's revelation. It started much earlier.

It started the day I gave birth to my daughter at age 18 and lost my womb in the process. I share this story in my first book, Transformed from Pain to Purpose. There is a particular grief that comes with losing something the world ties so tightly to womanhood. Something that feels, in the deepest and most primal way, like it defines what you are capable of producing — what you are capable of being. And when that loss happened, something shifted in the story I told myself about who I was and what I was worth.

The question that began that day was: *Why me?*

And underneath that question was a conclusion I didn't even realize I had reached: God must not love me.

Because if He did, why would He allow that to be taken away from me? Why would He allow that loss, and then the next one, and then the one after that? Why would a woman trying to do everything right keep experiencing setbacks?

I began to see myself as barren. Not just physically. Spiritually. Purposefully. Fundamentally barren.

When you believe you are barren, you do one of two things. You give up. Or you perform harder.

My pattern became to perform harder. Then I'd give up. Then I'd overachieved again. Then I'd burn out. I cycled between striving and collapse for years, each time believing the next push would finally quiet the lie. I pushed and built and sacrificed — not even to earn love anymore, but to prove I could produce as a woman. That the barrenness was a lie. That God hadn't made a mistake.

But performing to disprove a lie you haven't yet named is exhausting. Because the lie doesn't care how hard you work. It just moves the goalpost.

The Narrative Underneath Everything

Here is what I know now that I could not see then: the story was never true. I was never barren. I was bearing fruit. Just not always in the ways I could see or measure. Not always in the ways the world would recognize. The fruit was in the women I touched. The words I wrote. The songs I created in the middle of my breaking. The daughter I raised — fully, fiercely, with everything I had.

> *The fruit was in me, becoming.*

But you can't see the fruit when you are staring at the lie. It's hard to behold the beauty of the fruit when you're still focusing on the basket of your brokenness. And I had been staring at that lie for so long it had started to look like the truth.

Maybe yours has too. Maybe your narrative isn't "barren". Maybe it's unworthy. Not enough. Or too much. Or always abandoned. Or meant to struggle. Whatever the lie is — it is a lie. And healing the broken mirror begins with being willing to say that out loud. To hold it up to the light. To stop letting it run things from the shadows. Because a lie only has power in the dark. The moment you drag it into the open and look at it clearly, it begins to lose its grip.

FRAMEWORK: REWRITING THE NARRATIVE

The lies we believe about ourselves don't leave on their own. They have to be consciously identified, examined, and replaced with truth. This five-step process is your mirror work.

Step 1: Name the Core Lie:

Write down the deepest negative belief you hold about yourself. Not the watered-down version. The raw one. The one that whispers when you're alone. (Examples: I am not enough. I am cursed. I am unlovable. God is disappointed in me.)

Step 2: Face It and Trace Its Origin:

Where did this belief come from? A specific event? A person? A season? A wound? The lie didn't originate in you, it was planted. Name the source as clearly as you can.

Step 3: Cross-Examine the Lie

Put the lie on trial. Ask: What actual evidence supports this? What evidence contradicts it? What would I say to a friend who believed this about herself? Most lies collapse under honest examination.

Step 4: Write the Counter-Truth:

For every lie, write a truth. Not a positive affirmation you don't believe, a rooted, scriptural, evidence-based truth. (Example: I am not cursed. I am covered. God is not disappointed; He is pursuing me through every season.)

Step 5: Speak It Daily:

For 21 days, speak the counter-truth out loud every morning before you pick up your phone. Not once. Three times. Your voice carries authority over your own narrative. Use it.

This is not a one-time exercise. Deep lies were built over years — they don't dissolve in a day. Be patient with yourself. Keep returning to the truth until the truth becomes louder than the lie.

What Forgiveness Actually Looked Like

I want to be honest with you about something.

Forgiveness, of yourself, of God, of the people and circumstances that wounded you — is not a prayer you say once and feel better. At least it wasn't for me. For me, forgiveness looked like grief. Real, ugly, unperformed grief. Anger that I had to let myself feel before I could let go. A reckoning with all the time I had spent living inside a story that was never mine.

And then…music.

While navigating the deepest, most honest season of my life, I wrote three songs. Not for a platform. Not for an audience. I wrote them the same way I had always found my way home — through the words and melodies in my head, the piano, through the part of me that speaks more clearly in music than in words.

The last one I wrote was called *Becoming Me.*

And in it I wrote these lyrics: *I was chasing echoes, living in disguise. Wore a thousand faces, believed a thousand lies. Gave away my pieces trying to belong, but somewhere deep inside I knew it all felt wrong.*

Then came the turn. The moment the mirror started to heal.

"I heard a whisper in the silence. A voice that sounded just like me. She said — you've wandered far enough now. Come back home to me. Come back home to me."

The voice that called me home was mine. The me that was created in the mind of God before the world ever got to name me or wound me or form me into something smaller than I was made to be.

Home was never a place outside of me. Home was always me. Home is YOU. The woman God designed from the beginning. The one who knows who she is and whose she is. Maybe you needed to read that sentence a few times. That's okay. Read it again.

Faith Rebuilt from the Inside Out

I need to talk about what happened to my faith in Belize. Because I think it might be happening to yours too, if it hasn't already.

For most of my life, I related to God the way I related to everything and everyone else: as a performance. Do the right things. Check the right boxes. Pray enough. Serve enough. Show up to church enough. And maybe, just maybe, He will be pleased with me. What's interesting is that I'm a daddy's girl and never really had issues with my father's approval for anything, *outside of the softball field.* My dad never made me feel unloved. So, my distorted lens of God wasn't rooted in my relationship with him. It was rooted in something deeper. Wounds from other places. An orphan mindset that had taken up residence long before I had the language to identify it.

But what do you do with a God who doesn't seem pleased no matter how hard you perform? What do you do when you've done everything right and the loss and pain keeps coming anyway? You either keep pretending. Or you get honest.

In Belize, and even after I came back to the Unites States, I got honest. Honest with myself about my faith and the beliefs that had been handed to me without my examination. I watched my dad — a man who loves Jesus deeply — struggle to call on a God outside of himself to heal what was happening in his body, while not yet understanding the mental and spiritual work his own healing required. Not yet realizing the power he had been given to participate in his own restoration. And in watching him, I recognized myself.

I had been doing the same thing. Reaching upward and outward for a God I had never learned to find within. Not truly examining my beliefs. Not sitting with the hard questions. Performing faith instead of living it.

Something shifted. Not away from God, but toward Him. Toward a truer, deeper, more honest version of what faith could be.

A faith that didn't require performance to be real. A faith that held space for mystery and questions and grief. A faith that looked at my broken mirror and said: I see you. All of you. And I have always loved what I see.

That is the God I found on the other side of the performance. And He was never the one who was disappointed in me.

I was the one who had been hiding from Him.

Seeing Yourself the Way God Does

So, what does the healed mirror look like?

It looks like a woman who can stand in front of her reflection and see someone who was known before she was formed. It looks like releasing the story that God is disappointed in you and replacing it with the truth that He has been pursuing you through every season. Even the ones that felt like abandonment. Even the ones you are still trying to make sense of.

It looks like forgiving yourself not for being broken, but for believing the lie that broken meant you're unloved.

It looks like telling the truth out loud, maybe for the first time: I do not actually believe I am enough. And letting that be the beginning rather than the ending.

You are not cursed. You are not unworthy. You are not behind. You are not barren. You are not too much or too little or too late.

You are a woman in the middle of her becoming. In the middle of bearing fruit. And becoming requires breaking. Not as punishment, as preparation.

The version of you that God knew before you were formed — she
never stopped being worth knowing.

"I praise you because I am fearfully and wonderfully made."
— Psalm 139:14

REFLECT

What is the story — the lie — that has been looking back at you in the mirror? Where did it begin?

____

____

____

____

In what ways have you been performing for God rather than resting in Him?

____

____

____

____

What would it mean to hear the voice that calls you home and recognize it as your own?

____

____

____

____

If God knew you before you were formed, what do you think God knew?

PART TWO

THE RECLAMATION

Rebuilding Identity from the Inside Out

CHAPTER FOUR
BORN, NOT FORMED

*You were not assembled by the world's opinions of you. You were
born whole, original, and already known.*

You have done the hardest thing.

Not the hardest thing you will ever do, this journey is long
and it will ask more of you before it is finished. But in terms of
what most women spend their entire lives avoiding? You just did it.
You stopped. You looked. You told the truth.

You sat in the unraveling. You named the roles and the labels
and the breaking points. You looked at the stories you had been
carrying, the wounds that became your worldview, the losses that
became your identity, and you told the truth about them. Not the
polished version you share at dinner or the edited version you post
online. The real version. The one that lives in the quiet spaces of 2
a.m. when there is nothing left to distract you from yourself.

You traced the breaking all the way back to its origin. You sat
with the grief of it. The real grief. The kind that had no casserole
and no flowers and no one quite knowing what to say. The invisible

kind. The kind that doesn't get a funeral because the world can't see what you lost, only you know what it cost you to keep going.

That is not a small thing. That is an act of profound courage.

Because here is what most women do instead: they keep moving. They stay busy enough that the questions never catch up. They pour into everyone around them and call it purpose. They perform strength so convincingly that eventually even they believe it. They live their entire lives at the surface, capable, impressive, exhausted, and they never once stop long enough to ask what is underneath all of it?

You stopped. You asked. You stayed when every part of you wanted to run.

That takes more courage than most women ever give themselves credit for. And I want you to receive that before we go any further.

Now we move into something different. Not easier, just different. Because this part of the work is not about excavating what was broken. It is about building what is real. It is about learning to live from the inside out instead of the outside in. It is about choosing, daily and on purpose, the woman you were always meant to be, rather than the one the world shaped you to become. The one that wore the costume so long she forgot it wasn't her skin.

This is the Reclamation. And it begins with the most foundational question of everything that follows: not *who did I become*, but *who was I always?*

When you strip everything away, and I mean everything — what's left? No title. No role. No relationship that needs you. No one to perform for.

> *Just you.*

Sitting with that question is one of the most uncomfortable things a woman who has spent her whole life being something for somebody else can do. Because most of us have never tried it. And the ones who have, know that the first thing you feel when you finally get still enough is not peace.

It's boredom.

And then, if you stay long enough, something else. Something that doesn't announce itself. It doesn't come with a breakthrough moment or a dramatic revelation. It comes the way morning light comes. Slowly. Almost without your noticing. Until suddenly the room is different and you realize: she was here the whole time.

When I sat at that lagoon in Belize, I wasn't a brand. I wasn't a caregiver or a mother, or a mentor. I wasn't the strong one or the broken one or the one trying to hold it all together.

I was just Tacondra.

And honestly? I didn't know what to do with her without everything else. I had been so many things for so many people for so long that just being, with no role attached, no one to tend to like that, no performance to maintain — felt foreign. Almost wrong. Like I had shown up somewhere without my credentials and didn't know how to explain myself.

I sat with the boredom. I let it be uncomfortable. I cried. I comforted myself. I even allowed myself to feel all the emotions I had suppressed. The sadness for the years I had lost inside the performance, and the strange, tentative relief of finally being allowed to put it down. Both things were true at the same time. And I let them be.

Maybe you know this feeling. Maybe you've had a version of your own lagoon — not necessarily a body of water in another country, but a moment. A season. A day where the noise finally stopped long enough for something uncomfortable to surface in you. Maybe it was a long drive where you turned the music off and surprised yourself with what came up. Maybe it was the first morning after a relationship ended, or a job dissolved, or a chapter closed, and you lay there in the unfamiliar silence wondering who you were now that the thing that defined your days was just... gone.

Maybe you haven't had that moment yet. Maybe you have been moving too fast, too full of purpose and obligation and forward motion for it to catch you. If that is you, I want to say something: it is coming. And when it arrives, I don't want you to be afraid of it. I don't want you to reach for your phone or your calendar or your next project to fill it. I want you to sit in it the way I sat at that lagoon. Because what is waiting for you on the other side of the silence is not emptiness.

It is you. The original one. And she has been trying to get a word in for a long time.

And then slowly, something began to resurface.

Not all at once. In pieces. The way things come back to you when you finally stop running from yourself.

Childhood memories of bare feet in the grass. The specific softness of it. Laying on my back looking up at clouds, searching for shapes — a cow, a dog, something ridiculous — with nowhere to be and no one to impress. The uncomplicated joy of my pets curled up against me who simply loves me for no reason at all, who doesn't need me to be anything other than present.

And then, underneath all of that, my creativity. The raw kind. The kind that existed before anyone told me whether I was good at anything. The kind that has no audience and needs none. The kind that doesn't ask permission and doesn't wait for applause. The kind that doesn't come from hustling, discipline, strategy or a content calendar, it just moves through you the way breath moves. Not because you decided to breathe. Because it is simply what you were made to do.

I had not lost it. I had buried it. Under years of survival, performance and proving. And it had been down there the whole time, patient as anything, waiting for me to get quiet enough to remember.

For me, that creativity led me straight back to where I had always belonged.

To ME.

That woman I found at the lagoon was not built from nothing though. She had been shaped. By life, yes. By loss and survival, yes. But also, by beauty. By the women who walked before her and left something worth carrying. There is a particular kind of woman who shaped me more than almost anyone else. Not through instruction or intention, but simply through the extraordinary act of being fully herself in front of me. And for a long time, I did not understand the difference between being shaped by someone and becoming them. Between honoring an influence and disappearing into it.

That distinction changed everything.

Shaped By Her but Not Her

The women who shape us are gifts. But we were not meant to become them. We were meant to be informed by them, and then to go find what is ours. The version of us that no one else can replicate. The one that existed before we ever laid eyes on the woman we admired.

I want to intentionally pause for a moment to tell you about my aunt. If you know me personally, you've probably heard me talk about her. I've written about her in my first book and explained how I grew up around her the most as a little girl.

She is remarkable. The kind of woman who walks into a room and changes the environment just by being in it. She has had a profound impact on my life —on how I carry myself, how I show up in the world, my style and taste when it comes to fashion, material things, and more. I love her tremendously.

What is fascinating and a little terrifying at the same time, is that even during the seasons of my adult life when I wasn't spending much time with her at all, her essence was still very much present in me. I didn't have to be around her for her influence to show up. It had already taken root.

It showed up in the way I decorated my home. The way I walked into a room. The things I was drawn to, the way I carried myself, the standards I held, even the way I spoke. She was woven into me in ways I hadn't fully examined. And then one day, she came to visit my home in Texas. She walked through the door and looked around. She looked at me. She saw herself. In my walls, in my taste, in the way I dressed and even how I had arranged my space. There were other encounters where she'd just stop and look at me and say,

"Yep, you're definitely my seed." Without a word being said sometimes, we both felt it.

It was almost unsettling. Not because there was anything wrong with what she saw, but because it raised the question neither of us would say out loud:

How much of this is me — and how much of this is her?

But here is what I had to eventually reckon with: when people would see me, they would see her. And for a long time, I thought that was a compliment. It still is. But underneath it was a question I wasn't ready to ask myself: if people see her when they look at me, then where am I? Who am I beyond her image?

I had been borrowing her identity without realizing it. Modeling her essence, mostly unintentionally, and carrying her energy. Presenting her image beautifully and convincingly while still searching for my own underneath it. And here is the lesson I want you to receive from that:

> *It is okay to be shaped by the women who came before you. It is okay to admire someone so deeply that a little of them lives in how you show up. That is not a flaw — that is love. That is legacy in action.*

But there is a thin line. And the line is this: you can model after someone. You cannot build your identity on their blueprint. You cannot make their approval the measure of who you are. Because the moment their approval becomes your compass, you have quietly handed over the authorship of your own story. And one day — it might be gradual, or it might be a sudden flash of clarity in a mirror, or it might be someone calling you by a name that isn't yours — you will look up and realize you have become them. Not you. And the woman you were born to be has been standing quietly in the corner, waiting for you to notice her.

That is not an indictment of the person you modeled after. It is a wake-up call about the work you've still got to do.

Your identity cannot be built on someone else's foundation, no matter how beautiful that foundation is. It will never be yours. And deep down, you will always know the difference.

Born Identity vs. Formed Identity

Before you can choose something different, you must be able to recognize what you have been living in. And the tricky thing about the formed identity is that it does not announce itself. It does not feel like a performance from the inside.

It feels like you.

It feels like waking up in the morning and immediately calculating. Before your feet hit the floor, your brain is already running the list: What needs to get done today? Who needs what from me? What am I behind on? What do I need to deliver to maintain the version of myself that everyone is counting on? You mistake this for responsibility. For maturity. For being a good woman. But underneath it is something else entirely — the constant, low-grade anxiety of a woman who does not know who she is without something to prove.

It feels like saying yes when your whole body is screaming no and not even noticing the disconnect anymore, because you have overridden that inner signal so many times that it barely registers.

It is just background noise now.

It feels like doing something loving and then immediately monitoring the reaction. Not for appreciation exactly. But for confirmation. That you are enough. That you are loved. That you are seen. That your existence is justified by what you just gave. You would never call it that. But that is what the monitoring is for.

It feels like being in a room full of people who love you and feeling utterly alone — because not one of them knows the real version of you. They know the curated version. The one you assembled for this context. And you have been in that room so long that you have started to wonder if the real version even exists anymore.

That is the formed identity. Exhausting in a way that has no name, because you cannot point to any single thing that is wrong. Everything looks fine. From the outside, everything looks impressive. And yet something underneath it keeps tapping. Quietly. Persistently.

A woman who knows — in her bones — that this is not the whole story.

What Living from Your Born Identity Actually Feels Like

I want to describe what it felt like at that lagoon in Belize, because it is the closest I can get to putting words to what born identity feels like from the inside.

It felt like the absence of calculation. I woke up with no list running. No one to perform myself for. And at first — like I told you — that felt like emptiness. Like something was wrong. My formed identity had been so loud for so long that the silence of it felt like a malfunction.

But then, slowly, something else surfaced. Not goals. Not a to-do list. Just noticing. I noticed the way the light hit the water. I noticed that I wanted to hum something. I noticed that there was a melody in my head that had been there for years, waiting for a quiet enough moment to be heard.

And I followed it. Not because it was productive. Not because anyone was watching. Not because it would build a platform or prove anything. Just because it was mine. And something in me recognized it as mine without anyone having to tell me.

That is the born identity. It is the part of you that knows without being told. That recognizes home without a map. That moves toward certain things and away from others — not because of strategy, approval, or survival — but because something at your core quietly understands: this is me. This is actually, genuinely, originally me.

It does not feel triumphant, at least not at first. It feels quieter than that.

It feels like setting down something heavy you did not even know you were carrying.

The Distinction That Changes Everything

Your formed identity is who you became. It is the self you constructed — consciously and unconsciously — from everything that happened to you, everything that was done to you, everything you were told about yourself, and everything you learned to do to survive it. It contains real parts of you. It was not built in bad faith.

Much of it was built in love, in grief, in necessity, in the simple human need to belong.

But it was built from the outside in.

Your born identity is who you already were. Before the forming started. Before the first label was assigned and the first performance was rewarded and the first wound taught you what it cost to be fully yourself in a room that was not ready for you.

"Before I formed you in the womb I knew you."
— Jeremiah 1:5

God knew you before your body existed. Before your parents named you. Before anyone had a single expectation of you. That means your purpose did not arrive through what you survived or earned. Your purpose was born into you. And no wound, no loss, no borrowed identity, no decade of survival could remove it from you.

Unless you allow it.

The work of this book — and the work of our life — is learning to tell the difference between the two. Not to destroy the formed identity. Not to pretend it did not serve you in the seasons when you needed it. But to stop letting it run the show. To stop letting survival drive a life that was made for something far greater than surviving.

Because here is what I know from the other side of that unraveling: the born identity never left. It went quiet, yes. It got buried under years of performance and adaptation and survival. But it was always there. Tapping. Sending you those unmistakable moments of recognition — when you picked something up that felt like home or stood in a moment of total authenticity and thought: there she is.

She has always been there. The work is simply learning to let her lead.

FRAMEWORK: BORN VS. FORMED IDENTITY MAPPING

This two-column exercise helps you visually separate what is authentically yours from what was constructed in response to life. You will need a journal and about 30 minutes of uninterrupted time.

Step 1: Draw Two Columns:

Label the left column: FORMED (who I became). Label the right column: BORN (who I already was).

Step 2: Fill the Formed Column:

Write everything in the left column that you built in response to your life — behaviors you adopted to survive, roles you took on to be accepted, beliefs about yourself that came from wounds or other people's words.

Step 3: Fill the Born Column:

In the right column, write the things that have always been true about you before the performance started. Your natural gifts. The things you loved as a child before the world had opinions. The way you think, create, connect. The longings that never fully went away.

Step 4: Notice the Gaps:

Where do the two columns contradict each other? Where have you been living from your formed column when your born column is trying to speak? Circle every contradiction.

Step 5: Make a Declaration:

For each contradiction, write one sentence that chooses the born column. For example: I was formed to believe I need approval. But I was born to lead from conviction. Say each declaration out loud.

This is a living document. Return to it as you move through the book. Your born column should grow larger the further you go.

Finding Your Way Back

You start by paying attention to what feels like you when no one is watching.

Not what looks good. Not what's productive. What feels like home. What makes time disappear. What you would do even if no one ever saw it, applauded it, or called it valuable.

For me it was piano. The thing I set down on a softball field that had been waiting patiently for me to come back to it for decades.

Ask yourself: Before anyone told me who to be, who was I? What did I love before I learned to perform? Whose identity have I been borrowing and what have I left behind of my own to carry it?

You don't have to rebuild everything at once. You just have to start building from the inside out — from the truth of who you were made to be.

She has been waiting. And she is ready to be found.

REFLECT

Whose identity have you been borrowing and what did it cost you to carry it?

____

____

____

____

What is the gap between the image you present and the substance underneath it?

____

____

____

____

What would it mean to stop modeling someone else's essence and start embodying your own?

____

____

____

____

**What is one thing that is purely, originally, irreducibly you —
that no one gave you and no one can take away?**

CHAPTER FIVE

THE OTHER SIDE OF THE MIRROR

A legacy is not a line of women who look like you. A legacy is a line of women who are fully themselves because of you.

You already know her. In the last chapter, she was the woman whose home reflected her aunt's taste, whose walk carried her energy, whose mirror showed a borrowed reflection.

There is another woman in this story. We have spent time talking about the woman who borrows. Who models after someone she admires, who builds herself in another woman's image, who one day looks in the mirror and realizes the reflection staring back belongs to someone else.

But what about the woman on the other side?

What about the one being borrowed from?

This chapter is for her.

And if you have been building anything — a platform, a ministry, a brand, a family, a community, a life that other women are watching — this chapter is for you too. Because at some point on this journey, you will find yourself standing on both sides of that mirror. And you need to know what to do when you get there.

The Weight of Influence

I did not always understand the weight of what I was carrying.

There came a point in my journey when I realized the influence I possess. I began noticing how women were modeling after me. Not just women I had intentionally poured into, but followers, women I crossed paths with briefly, who were taking pieces of me and building themselves from them. My hairstyles. My words. My style. My theories. My ideas. My way of showing up. My aesthetic. My energy.

And at first, I won't lie, it was admirable. There is something deeply humbling about realizing that the way you carry yourself has become a reference point for someone else. That your presence left enough of an impression that a woman walked away from it and said I want some of that. But then I began to see the other side of it.

I watched women take my words and try to teach them before they had lived them. I watched them adopt my framework before they had walked through the process the framework came from. I watched them model the look, the language, the posture — without having done the interior work that gave those things their weight. And that is when I understood something that changed how I think about influence entirely.

It is admirable to be someone's model. It is dangerous if that model hasn't taught them to find themselves.

Because what I was watching — what made me unsettled in a way I couldn't immediately name — was women who were looking the part without being the part. Who were presenting the image without having embodied the identity. Who were teaching what I and so many others before me had earned through fire, without having stood in the fire themselves.

You Cannot Be Duplicated

Here is what I want you to understand about yourself first and about your influence, whether you feel influential or not:

You cannot be duplicated.

Not your full self. Not the complete, integrated, born-identity version of you that was formed in the mind of God before the world told you who to become. No one can replicate that. No one can borrow it, copy it, or model it closely enough to possess it.

Identity is not a style. It is not an aesthetic. It is not a set of theories or a collection of mannerisms or a particular way of walking into a room. Those things can be observed and imitated. But identity — the real thing, the born thing — is foundational. It lives on the inside. And it cannot be transferred by imitation alone.

You can borrow someone's style and language. You can borrow their beliefs or frameworks. And none of that is inherently wrong, because we are all shaped by the people we admire. That is part of how growth works.

But you cannot borrow someone's identity. And you should never try to build yours on their foundation.

Why? Because a foundation that is not yours will eventually crack under the weight of your actual life. Their blueprint was not built for you. It was built for her — for her specific story, her specific wounds, her specific calling, her specific relationship with God. When the storms come — and they will come — you need to be standing on ground that belongs to you.

"If you don't know who you are, you don't know who you aren't. And that gap is where borrowed identity takes root."
— Sheryll Broadnax

The Danger of Unchecked Influence

I want to be honest about something that made me deeply reflective when I began to see this pattern — both in myself and in the women around me.

When women model after you — or after anyone — without doing their own interior work, without knowing who they are at their core, they do not just borrow your strengths. They borrow your presentation of your strengths. And there is a significant difference between the two.

Your strength came from somewhere. It came from a process. From a fire you walked through. From a season of being broken and choosing to rebuild. From years of doing the inner work that eventually produced the outer fruit. The authority in your voice is not accidental — it is the residue of lived experience.

When someone models the voice without walking the journey, they are carrying weight they are not yet equipped to hold. And it will show. Not always immediately. But eventually, the lack of congruence between how they show up in public and who they are in private will surface.

There must be congruence.

That word — congruence — is everything. It means that who you are on the stage matches who you are off it. That what you teach is what you live. That the image you present to the world is anchored in a reality that exists when no one is watching. A woman with congruence does not perform her wholeness. She inhabits it. And that is the gift you want to leave the women who watch you. Not a copy of your image. Not a replica of your style. But the urgent, non-negotiable understanding that they must do the work of finding out who they are before they try to carry what you carry.

What True Legacy Looks Like

A legacy is not a line of women who look like you.

A legacy is a line of women who are fully themselves because of you.

There is a profound difference between the two. And I want you to sit with that — because in a world that celebrates influence and platforms and reach and followers, it is easy to measure your legacy by how many people are modeling after you. By how many women have adopted your language, your framework, your aesthetic.

But that is not legacy. That is not multiplication. That is replication. And replication, without identity, produces hollow vessels.

True legacy looks like the mentee who sat with you, absorbed your wisdom, felt your presence, and then went home and did the deep interior work of finding out who she was. Who took what you gave her not as an identity to wear, but as a lantern to help her find her own way in the dark.

True legacy looks like a younger woman who says not, "I want to be like her" — but "because of her, I became more fully myself."

That is the goal. That is what you are building toward every time you show up authentically, every time you choose congruence over performance, every time you refuse to present an image that is not backed by substance.

You are not just building a platform. You are setting a standard — for what it looks like to be a whole woman.

And the women watching you are learning not just from what you say, but from how you live. They are watching whether your private life matches your public voice. Whether you rest when you say rest matters. Whether you really do maintain boundaries when you say boundaries are beautiful. Whether the peace you speak about is one you possess.

That is the sermon that outlives every stage moment.

A Word to the Women Watching You Right Now

If there is a woman in your life —a mentee, a daughter, a younger sister, a follower — who you know is modeling after you, I want you to give her the greatest gift you can give:

Tell her who you are not just on the surface, but who you had to become. Tell her about the breaking. Tell her about the seasons where the image cracked and what was underneath it. Tell her about the work you did in private that produced the fruit she sees in public. Let her see the cake, not just the icing. Because if she only ever sees the finished product, she will try to skip the process. And the process is not optional.

Tell her that she cannot build her life on your foundation. That she is allowed to admire you, to be shaped by you, to carry pieces of your wisdom forward. But that her identity must come from within herself. From her own encounter with God. From her own unraveling and her own rebuilding. From her own lagoon in Belize, wherever that turns out to be for her.

Tell her: I am not the blueprint. I am the example that blueprints exist.

And then set her free to find her own.

FRAMEWORK: THE LEGACY BUILDER'S MIRROR

*This exercise is for the woman who leads, teaches, mentors, or influences —
whether she knows it or not. Before you can leave a healthy legacy, you must
examine the one you are currently building.*

Step 1: Name Your Watchers:

Write down 3–5 women you know are watching you, modeling after
you, consciously or not. These might be mentees, daughters, younger colleagues, or followers. Name them specifically.

Step 2: Audit Your Influence:

For each woman, ask honestly: What is she learning from watching
me? Is she learning how to be authentically herself — or how to
look like me? Is what she sees in me backed by the private work that
produced it?

Step 3: Check Your Congruence:

On a scale of 1–10, how congruent are you? How closely does the
woman you present publicly match the woman you are privately?
Where are the gaps and what is causing them?

Step 4: Set Her Free:

Write a letter — even if you never send it — to one woman who
has been modeling after you. Tell her what you want her to keep
from your influence and what you want her to leave behind. Tell her
who she is that is not you.

Step 5: Define Your Legacy Statement:

Complete this sentence: I want the women who come after me to be fully _______________ because of their time with me. Not more like me. More like themselves. Write that statement somewhere visible.

The most powerful thing you can model for the women watching you is not your success. It is your authenticity. Show them what it looks like to do the interior work. Let them see the process, not just the product.

The Other Side of the Mirror

My aunt never tried to make me her replica.

She simply lived. Fully, unapologetically, remarkably herself. And in doing so, she became a standard, not a template. The difference is everything. A standard says: this is what excellence looks like, now go find what it looks like for you. A template says: copy this exactly and you will arrive.

My aunt gave me a standard. And when she walked through my door and saw herself reflected in me, I believe what she felt was not pride of possession. It was something more beautiful than that.

It was the recognition that something of her lives on — not as a copy, but as an influence. As a seed that had taken root in different soil and grown into something that was, ultimately, its own tree.

That is the other side of the mirror.

Not a reflection. A new original.

And that is exactly what you are — regardless of who shaped you, who influenced you, who you have modeled after along the way.

You are not their reflection. You are a new original. And the world has been waiting for exactly that.

"For we are God's handiwork, created in Christ Jesus to do good works, which God prepared in advance for us to do."
— **Ephesians 2:10**

REFLECT

Who is watching you right now — modeling after you,
consciously or not — and what do you want them to learn from
observing your life?

What is the difference between the image you present publicly
and the reality of your private process? Is there congruence?

What do you want the women who come after you to carry from
your influence — and what do you want them to leave behind?

____

____

What would it look like to give the women watching you permission to be fully themselves rather than a version of you?

____

____

____

____

CHAPTER SIX

HOW TO REDISCOVER WHO YOU ARE

You don't have to remember who you were. Sometimes you get to discover her for the very first time.

How to Rediscover Who You Are

Identity work is not always a return to who you were. Sometimes it is discovering who you are… maybe for the very first time.

Not every woman has a thread to trace back to. Not every woman can close her eyes and find a childhood memory that points her home. Some grew up in environments where discovering what they loved was never safe, never encouraged, or simply never possible. Some performed for so long, and so young, that they genuinely do not know where the performance ends and the real person begins.

If that is you, I want you to know this: you do not need a memory to find yourself. You just need curiosity. And curiosity is always available to you.

The Permission Slip

Before we go any further, I want to give you something. Consider this your official permission slip to not know yet.

That's right. You do not have to walk into this season of rediscovery with a clear answer. You do not have to already know what you love, what lights you up, what your purpose is, or who you are outside of every role you have ever played. If you already know some of these things, great! But not knowing is not a failure. Not knowing is the beginning.

The women who struggle most in this season are the ones who treat rediscovery like a performance. Who put pressure on themselves to figure it out quickly, to have a beautiful answer, to arrive at their born identity on a timeline that makes sense to everyone watching. But rediscovery is not a performance. It is an exploration. And explorations do not have deadlines.

Give yourself the gift of not knowing and the freedom to find out.

Two Roads to Rediscovery

There are generally two ways women find their way back to themselves. Most women travel a little of both. The first road is remembering. Going back before the performance started and asking, what was true about me then? What did I love? What did I gravitate toward naturally, without anyone asking me to? What made me lose track of time? What did I do just because it felt right?

The second road is discovering. Trying things you have never tried. Going places you have never gone. Asking questions you have never asked yourself. Building a relationship with your own preferences, reactions, instincts, and curiosities as if you are meeting yourself for the first time because in many ways, you are. Neither road is better. Neither is easier. And for most women, the truest version of themselves lives somewhere at the intersection of both.

If You Do Have a Memory to Return To

Maybe you do have a thread, a thing you loved before the world got loud. Before the approval-seeking started. Before the performance took over.

Maybe it was art. Writing. Dancing. Cooking. Building things. Being in nature. Making people laugh. Leading. Teaching. Singing in the shower when nobody was listening. If something just came to mind, that is not an accident.

Here is what I want you to do with it:

Do not question it. Do not measure its value by whether it is practical, profitable, or impressive. Do not ask whether it makes sense for your season of life. Do not wonder if you are too old, too far gone, or too out of practice. Just go back to it.

Start small if you need to. Pick it up in a quiet Tuesday afternoon with no audience and no agenda. Let it be imperfect and rusty and wonderful. Let it remind you that you have always known exactly who you are, you just got busy for a while. That thread has been waiting. And it will welcome you home like you never left.

If You Don't Have a Memory

If you cannot find the thread — if childhood feels too distant to remember, too painful, or simply too blank to pull anything useful from — do not force it. You are simply starting from today.

And today is a perfectly valid place to start.

Practice paying attention. Pay attention to what draws you. What repels you. What makes you lean in. What makes you feel like you are finally in the right room. What makes you feel like you need to leave. Your born identity is not hiding in the past. It is alive in you right now, in your reactions, your instincts, your curiosities, your longings. You just have to start listening to her.

The Self-Discovery Map

What did my journey look like? I'm glad you asked. I have ADHD — so you can imagine it wasn't linear. I call it the "follow the yellow brick road" journey. I took personality tests. Explored my DNA and ancestry. I read more books. I questioned beliefs I'd held for years, including ones that were handed to me. Met people who pushed me past my own edges. Tried new things, took new roads, traveled to places that had everything to do with expansion. There is no checklist. No finish line you cross and then move on from. Think of it like a map, and like all good maps, it shows you possibilities, not destinations. You decide which roads to take, which ones to turn back from, and which ones to follow all the way through.

Work through these questions below slowly. In a journal. Over multiple sittings with no distractions.

PART ONE: What Already Stirs You

Start with what you already know, even if it is just a feeling. Ask yourself these questions and answer them truthfully. When you scroll through social media and feel a genuine "ughhh" of something — not jealousy exactly, but longing — what are people doing that triggers it? What life are you quietly wishing was yours? What topics do you read about, watch videos about, or talk about when no one has specifically asked for your opinion? When you are in a conversation and feel genuinely lit up — not performing, not being polite — what is being discussed?

What would you do tomorrow if money, time, skill level, and other people's opinions were completely removed from the equation? What have you started and stopped multiple times over the years, not because you didn't love it but because life got in the way? That thing that keeps finding its way back to you?

PART TWO: What Your Body Already Knows

Your body carries information your mind has not caught up to yet. These questions are designed to access it.

1. When you walk into certain spaces or environments — a music studio, a kitchen, a gym, a garden, a stage, a classroom, a forest, a city, a bookstore — which ones make your body relax in a specific way, like something in you recognizes it?

2. What activity makes time disappear for you? Not scroll time, intentional time. Where do you lose track of the clock because you are fully absorbed?

3. What do you do when you are celebrating something privately just for you, no one watching? That thing you reach for when you want to feel like yourself?

4. When you imagine your most alive self, not your most successful self, not your most impressive self, where is she? What is she doing? Who is she with?

5. What has your body been asking for that you have been too busy to give it? Rest. Movement. Creativity. Silence. Adventure. Connection. Community. Solitude?

PART THREE: What Comes Naturally

Sometimes who we are is so natural to us that we discount it entirely. We assume that if it comes easily, it can't be significant.

1. What do people consistently come to you for that you give away freely without even thinking about it?

2. What do you do effortlessly that you have watched others struggle with?

3. What kind of problems do you naturally gravitate toward solving in your own life, in other people's lives, in the world?

4. What do you notice in a room that other people walk right past? What do you see that others seem to miss?

5. If you could spend the next ten years working on one problem in the world, not for money, not for recognition, just because it matters deeply to you, what would it be?

PART FOUR: What You Have Never Tried but Keep Thinking About

Curiosity is the compass of the born identity. If something keeps showing up in your mind — a class, a trip, a skill, a creative pursuit, a type of community, a way of living — pay attention to it.

1. What is on your list of things you have always said *I'd love to try that someday*, and what has *someday* actually been waiting for?

2. What intimidates you in a way that also excites you? That specific combination of fear and interest is almost always pointing somewhere important.

3. If you could apprentice under anyone in the world for one year, not for a career, just to learn, who would it be and what would you want to learn?

4. What kind of woman do you secretly admire? The kind that makes you think *I wish I was more like that* — and what specific quality in her are you actually recognizing in yourself?

5. What would you try if you knew you absolutely could not fail at it and no one would ever find out you attempted it?

PART FIVE: What the World Needs That You Carry

Your born identity is not just about what you enjoy. It is about what you carry. What you are built to give. What the world is missing when you are not fully yourself in it.

1. What is the thing you wish existed in the world — a space, a resource, a conversation, a community — that you have never been able to find?

2. Whose story do you find yourself most drawn to? Which people, which journeys, which struggles resonate with you in a way that goes beyond sympathy?

3. What do you know from lived experience that you believe more people need to hear?

4. If you had a platform and everyone who needed to hear your message was listening, what would you say?

5. What kind of impact do you want to leave? Not the impressive answer, the true one?

Some More Practical Ways to Begin

Reading about rediscovery is one thing. Actually, stepping into it is another. Here are some practical ways to start, not all of them, just the ones that call to you.

Take yourself on a solo date. Once a week, take yourself somewhere with no agenda. A museum. A botanical garden. A new neighborhood. A craft store. A live music venue. A bookstore where you have never shopped before. Notice what draws you. Notice what you linger over. Notice what makes you feel like you belong there.

Try one new thing per month for three months. Not to become an expert. Not to perform a new interest. Just to explore. A pottery class. A hiking trail. A cooking lesson. A dance style. A new genre of book. A volunteer opportunity. A creative writing workshop. A language. Give each thing at least two genuine attempts before you move on.

Start a discovery journal. Not a gratitude journal. Not a manifestation journal. A discovery journal. Every day, write one thing you noticed about yourself. Something you liked, something that surprised you, something that stirred something, something that bored you into a stupor. Over time a portrait of the real you will emerge from the pages.

P.S. If you didn't already purchase one to go with this book, I have a discovery journal linked on my website! It's called, "Wholeness Unleashed: A Journal to Reflect, Renew, and Awaken the Woman Within".

No prompts, no daily tasks. Just blank pages for you to explore YOU. Or feel free to use your own personal journal!

Now, what I'm about to say might be a hard pill to swallow but pay attention to envy. Not the destructive kind, the quiet kind. Envy is one of the most honest things that points to something within you that needs to be addressed. When you feel that specific ache of, *she has something I want*…sit with it long enough to ask: what specifically is she doing that I want to be doing? That answer almost always points to a pressure or void in your life that's true. My advice? Deal with it before it deals with you.

Talk to the people who knew you before the performance. A childhood friend. A parent or sibling who remembers you young. A mentor who knew you before the titles. Ask them: what did you notice about me then that you think I've forgotten? What did I love that I don't seem to do anymore? What did I light up about? Let their memories supplement your own.

Spend time in silence. Real silence. Not background noise silence. The kind where you sit with yourself and do not immediately reach for your phone or a task or a distraction. The born identity speaks in the quiet. She has been trying to get a word in for years. Give her some room.

Travel somewhere unfamiliar, even locally. You do not have to go to Belize. You just have to go somewhere that does not already have expectations of you attached to it. A new city. A different part of your own city. A day trip somewhere you have never been. New environments strip away the performance because no one there knows what role you are supposed to be playing.

The Woman at the End of the Map

Here is what I want you to know as you begin this journey of rediscovery. The woman waiting at the end of this map, the one you are working toward, the one you have been excavating through every exercise and every honest question and every new thing you dare to try. She is not a stranger.

She is not someone you have never met. She is the woman you have always been underneath everything. She has been in every room you have ever walked into. She has been present in every relationship, every season, every moment of your life. You have felt her in the times you were most alive, most honest, most yourself. In the moments before you remembered to perform. She does not need to be created. She does not need to be constructed or engineered or figured out.

She just needs to be allowed.

So, allow her. Slowly. Imperfectly. With curiosity and patience and the kind of grace you would extend to a woman you loved deeply and wanted desperately to see become her most authentic self.

You are coming home.

That is exactly what is happening.

CHAPTER SEVEN

STOP PERFORMING.
START BECOMING.

Part of the becoming is simply being. Not doing. And that is one of the hardest things most people can do because you're so used to go, go, go that you don't know how to just be.

At some point, understanding is not enough.

You can identify the performance. You can name the formed identity. You can trace the broken mirror all the way back to its origin. You can sit at a lagoon in Belize and have the most honest conversation with yourself you've ever had.

And then you must come home. Back to real life. Back to responsibilities and relationships and rhythms that were there before the breakthrough. Back to a world that will, if you let it, pull you right back onto the hamster wheel before the suitcase is even unpacked. So, the question becomes: how do you actually live differently?

The First Thing That Changed

I'm not going to give you a ten-step program. I'm going to tell you what I did. The first concrete thing that changed after Belize was simple. Almost embarrassingly simple.

I went to Orange Theory.

Yep, I went to a fitness studio to work out. *Shout out to my OT ladies!*

Not for anyone else. Not to look a certain way or prove anything to anybody. I went because for the first time in longer than I could remember, I was putting my own health — my physical body, my mental state, my energy — first. Not after everyone else's needs were met. Not in the margins of a life already overfull. *First.*

That sounds small. It is not small. For a woman who had spent years pouring herself out for everyone around her, choosing herself first, even in that one small way, was a revolution. I continued leaning into my creativity. New ideas. New visions. New dreams.

And I also removed from my life what no longer served the version of me I was becoming.

Becoming begins in the smallest, most honest choices you make when no one is asking anything of you.

Who's Behind the Wheel?

I want to be honest with you: the performance doesn't disappear just because you've named it. It still shows up. It shows up in my life today at times. Because truthfully, there is a level of performance in almost everything we do. The question is not am I ever performing? The question is: who is behind the wheel?

Is it your born identity — the woman who knows who she is, makes decisions from wholeness, and shows up because she genuinely wants to? Or is it the old, formed identity — driven by fear, approval-seeking, the need to be needed?

Because here is what the old identity does: it disguises itself. It shows up dressed as responsibility. As love. As strength. It says things like I'm just being dependable or I'm just showing up for the people I love.

Awareness is the first act of becoming. You cannot change what you will not see.

Once you catch the old identity sliding into the driver's seat, you have the power to make a different choice. Not a perfect choice. Not always the easiest one. But a conscious one. Made from your new identity rather than your old survival patterns.

Get Some Icing Up Underneath That Cake

Part of shifting who is behind the wheel is being honest about something that most high-achieving women are reluctant to admit: we become masterful at the exterior long before we fully develop the interior. The performance was not just something we did in certain rooms, it became the foundation we built our entire identity on. And eventually, the gap between what you present and what you actually possess can start doing damage.

Here is something that was said to me by someone I highly respect and I now say it to women, and I want to say it to you:

> *Get some icing up underneath that cake.*

Because what I realized about myself, and what I see in a lot of women often, is that we become masterful at presentation long before we develop substance. We learn early how to look the part. How to carry ourselves with confidence we haven't fully earned yet. How to speak the language of wholeness while privately still in pieces. And for a season, it works. People are drawn to the image. They applaud the presentation. They say things like *she has it all together* and *I want to be like her.*

But here's what nobody tells you about building a life on image: it is exhausting to maintain. And it is fragile. Because the image is only as strong as what is underneath it.

That is the icing and the cake.

The icing is what everyone sees, the polished exterior, the curated presence, the performance of a woman who has figured it out. And listen, there is nothing wrong with beautiful icing. Presentation matters. How you carry yourself matters. The care you put into how you show up in the world matters.

But if there is nothing underneath it — if the cake itself is hollow— eventually, the whole thing collapses. And no one wants to bite into something beautiful with nothing inside… *flavorless at that!*

It's happened to me and I've seen it happen to others. I have seen women build entire platforms, brands, and ministries on borrowed revelation. Teaching theories and principles they have not yet lived. Preaching healing they have not yet walked through. Presenting confidence they do not yet possess. And for a while, no one notices. The icing looks so good that people assume the cake must be there.

Women are perceptive. We can feel when someone is performing their "anointing" rather than living it. We can sense when the words are right, but the embodiment is missing. There is an emptiness to borrowed authority that no amount of polish can fully conceal. *You can only parrot someone else's revelations for so long before the gap between what you project and what you embody becomes impossible to ignore.*

And that gap, that space between the image and the reality, is one of the loneliest places a woman can live. Because you are surrounded by people who think they know you, and not one of them really does. You are receiving applause for a version of yourself you privately know is not the whole truth. And instead of feeling full, the applause just makes the emptiness within louder.

That is what happens when the icing is doing all the work.

So, what does it look like to put some cake up underneath the icing? It looks like doing the private work that the public will never see. It looks like sitting with your own wounds and patterns before you try to speak to someone else's. It looks like building a relationship with God that exists outside of the performance of faith. In the quiet, ugly and honest moments, in the places where no one is watching and you are still choosing truth. It looks like knowing yourself deeply enough that when you open your mouth to teach, lead, or guide, what comes out has roots. It has weight. It has the kind of authority that only comes from lived experience.

The image impresses. The identity endures. One gets you in the room. The other determines what happens once you're there.

The woman who walks in with a powerful image turns heads. But the woman who walks in with a rooted identity changes rooms and environments. There is a difference…and the people in that room will feel it before they can name it.

So, when building the brand, be mindful about doing the internal work. Before you teach the framework, live the framework. Before you declare the healing, do the healing. Put some substance underneath the surface. Build the cake first. Because the world does not need more beautiful icing on empty layers. *It needs women who are as whole on the inside as they appear on the outside.* And that kind of wholeness? It cannot be borrowed. It cannot be modeled after someone else. It cannot be performed into existence.

Identity isn't borrowed. It's built. From the inside out. From knowing yourself, trusting yourself, and choosing yourself even when it costs you something.

And when you build it that way…slowly, honestly, from the inside out — what you bring to every room you walk into is not a presentation. It is a presence.

And presence? *That* outlives image and performance every time.

The image impresses. The identity endures. One gets you in the room. The other determines what happens once you're there.

The Savior Has Left the Building

One of the most liberating, and most uncomfortable, things I learned on this journey was this:

It is not your responsibility to save people.

For those of us who built our identities around being the strong one, the fixer, that sentence feels like a betrayal. But here is what I learned about the savior complex that you don't hear often: when you position yourself as someone's savior, you are not just helping them. You are placing yourself in control of their life. Their healing. Their decisions. Some would call it a subtle form of emotional control, keeping others dependent because it keeps you feeling needed and necessary. It is worth examining honestly. I know, you might not view it that way but do some research on this. You'll be surprised at what you'll find.

When you let go of the need to save everyone around you, you stop depleting yourself in ways that leave you with nothing. And you give the people around you back their own agency, their own journey, their own opportunity to find their strength.

Let go of your need to be needed. That sentence alone changed my life.

The Beauty of No

I want to talk about boundaries, but not in the way the internet talks about them. Not as a wall you build to keep people out. I want to talk about boundaries as an act of self-honor.

Every yes is a no to something else. You may not know what that something else is in the moment. But it is always true.

When you say yes to staying late, you are saying no to rest. When you say yes to carrying someone else's emotional weight, you are saying no to your own peace. No one tells you this. We are taught to say yes. To be available, accommodating, always showing up.

No is a complete sentence. You do not have to explain it, justify it, or apologize for it. You are allowed to say no simply because the answer is no.

Value your *no* so deeply that your *yes* becomes sacred.

FRAMEWORK: THE DAILY BECOMING PRACTICE

Becoming is not a moment, it is a daily practice. These five practices, done consistently, rewire your patterns from performance-driven to identity-rooted. Start with one. Add more as they become natural.

Step 1: The Morning Check-In:

Before you pick up your phone each morning, ask yourself three questions: Who am I today, my born identity or my formed identity? What do I want to say yes to today that is truly mine? What do I need to protect today to stay aligned? Write one sentence in answer to each.

Step 2: The Yes/No Audit:

Once a week, review the commitments on your calendar. For each one, ask: Is this a yes from my born identity, or a yes from fear, obligation, or the need to be needed? For anything that falls in the second category, ask yourself what it would look like to renegotiate, reduce, or release it.

Step 3: The Belize Practice:

Once a day, even for ten minutes, practice going slow. No phone. No productivity. No agenda. Sit outside. Drive in silence. Drink your coffee without distraction. Let your mind wander. This is not wasted time. This is where your born identity speaks most clearly.

Step 4: The Creativity Return:

Identify one thing you loved before the performance started, something that is purely, originally yours. Schedule it once a week. Not because it's productive. Not because it leads anywhere. Simply because it is an act of belonging to yourself.

Step 5: The Driver's Seat Check:

Whenever you feel reactive, anxious, resentful, or depleted… pause and ask: Who is driving right now? Is this my born identity responding or my old, formed identity reacting? This single question, practiced daily, is more powerful than any other tool in this chapter.

You will not do all five perfectly. You will miss days. That is not failure, that is being human. The goal is not a perfect practice. The goal is a returning practice. Come back whenever you drift.

Go Slow. Breathe.

In Belize, I didn't understand at first why everything felt so different. And then I realized, nothing was rushing me. I could truly *REST*. There is a way of life built into the culture there. An insistence on the value of slowness. Of presence. Of breathing. *Go slow.*

Those two words undid something in me that years of hustle culture had wound tightly. In the United States, we live on a rat wheel. Spinning. Always spinning. Chasing the next achievement, the next milestone, the next level. And the wheel is seductive because it feels like purpose. But from the inside, it's exhausting. And it's one of the most effective ways the old performed identity stays in power. Because when you are always moving, always producing, you never have to sit still long enough to ask whether any of it is even *you.*

I'll be honest: coming back to the U.S. was hard. I eventually fell back into distraction. The pace catches you. Life catches you. I'm not standing here telling you I maintained perfect Belize energy in a Texas zip code. But what I carried back was the memory of what slow felt like. The reminder of what it felt like to breathe without an agenda. And I return to that place in my mind when I feel the wheel starting to spin too fast.

Being Before Doing

Here is one of the hardest things I have ever had to learn.

> *Becoming begins with being. Not doing.*

We are so conditioned to produce. To achieve. To have something to show for our time. That when someone tells us to just be — to sit in a moment without an agenda — it feels almost physically uncomfortable. Being looks like sitting in your backyard with your coffee and not picking up your phone. It looks like driving in silence instead of filling the car with noise. It looks like an afternoon with no plans and resisting the urge to fill it with productivity.

The woman you are becoming is not built in the doing. She is revealed in the *being*. In the stillness. In the spaces between the activity where you can finally hear yourself think.

You are not a human doing. You are a human being. And sometimes the most revolutionary thing you can do is simply be.

Becoming is not a destination. It is an ongoing, beautiful, sometimes surprising process of discovering who you truly are and giving her permission to keep showing up.

REFLECT

What is one small, concrete way you can choose yourself first this week?

____

____

____

____

Where does the old identity still try to take the wheel and what does it feel like when it does?

____

____

____

____

What are you currently saying yes to that is really a no to something more important?

____

____

____

____

When is the last time you just were — without doing, producing, or performing?

____

____

____

____

PART THREE
BE RADIANT

Living as the Woman You Were Born to Be

CHAPTER EIGHT

THE WOMAN WHO BELONGS TO HERSELF

If you don't know who you are, you will go looking for someone to tell you. And that is how you end up losing yourself — building your whole identity on the foundation of someone else's approval.

There is a version of you that has been waiting for permission. Permission to take up space. Permission to trust her own voice. Permission to stop hiding, stop apologizing, stop editing herself down to a size that makes everyone else comfortable. She has been waiting for someone, the right relationship, the right opportunity, the right season, to finally make her feel like she belongs.

But here is what I need you to understand before we go any further: *No one can give you what you have not first given yourself.*

If you do not belong to yourself, if you haven't done the work of knowing who you are, trusting what you feel, and choosing yourself even when it costs you, you will spend your whole life looking for someone else to do it for you.

And that is how you lose yourself. Not in one dramatic moment. But slowly, quietly, in a thousand small surrenders to someone else's approval.

The Danger of Looking Outside Yourself

When you don't know who you are, you go looking for someone to tell you. And when you outsource that answer, you hand someone else the pen to write your story. They will write it based on what they need from you, what fits into the version of their life where you make the most sense.

They will write a character. Not a woman.

Real belonging, the kind that actually sustains you, starts from the inside. It starts with knowing yourself well enough that you don't need someone else's validation to confirm that you are real, that you are worthy, that you have a right to be exactly who you are in every room you walk into.

You belong to yourself first. And from that place you can then choose the relationships and spaces that are worthy of your presence. Not the other way around.

What Self-Betrayal Actually Feels Like

Self-betrayal rarely announces itself. It doesn't show up at the door with a name tag. It slides in quietly, disguised as flexibility. As compromise. As being a good person who considers others.

But your body knows.

Your body keeps the score and tells the story you're avoiding. Betraying yourself looks like saying yes when every part of you is screaming no and swallowing the discomfort because it feels easier than the conversation. It looks like getting up and pushing through when your body is begging you to rest — until you crash, or burn out, or get sick in a way that forces the rest you refused to give yourself voluntarily.

It looks like silencing the thought that just told you the truth because the truth is inconvenient right now.

Learn that feeling. That is not anxiety. That is your born identity tapping you on the shoulder saying, this is not aligned. This is not us. Don't do this.

The People You Might Lose

I want to quickly address something directly because it needs to be said out loud. When you start belonging to yourself, some people will not like it. They were comfortable with the version of you that performed. The one who always said yes. The one who was always available for them. The one who made herself small so they could feel big. That version was easy to be around. Easy to take from.

The woman who belongs to herself is a different story. She has opinions. She has limits. She says no without a three-paragraph explanation. She doesn't do fake or foolishness. She takes up space unapologetically. She stops being available for things that cost her peace. Let me say this as gently and as directly as I know how: *that is not your responsibility to fix.*

The relationships that can only survive your smallness were never really built for you. They were built for your performance.

And as painful as it is to watch some of them shift or fall away, what you will find on the other side is something far more valuable. Relationships built on the real you. People who don't need you to be smaller. People who are not threatened by your wholeness but drawn to it. Those people exist. And you will not find them while you are still shrinking and performing.

FRAMEWORK: THE SELF-BELONGING COMMITMENT

Self-belonging is not a feeling; it is a daily practice of choosing yourself. These commitments, made in writing and renewed regularly, become the architecture of a life lived from the inside out.

Step 1: Write Down Your Non-Negotiables:

List five things you will no longer compromise about yourself — your time, your energy, your voice, your peace, your purpose. These are not preferences. These are the lines that define your belonging to yourself.

Step 2: Identify Your Self-Betrayal Patterns:

Name the three most common ways you betray yourself. (Examples: I say yes when I mean no. I over-explain my decisions. I shrink in rooms where I feel unseen. I give more than I have.) Write them down without judgment.

Step 3: Create Your Catch Phrase:

Choose one sentence you will say to yourself the moment you catch yourself betraying yourself. Something short, direct, and grounding. (Examples: Come back. This is not alignment. Choose her.) Practice saying it until it becomes instinctive.

Step 4: Build Your Return Ritual:

When you drift — and you will — what brings you back to yourself? For me it was working out, music, and stillness by water. For you it might be prayer, journaling, a walk, a song, silence. Name your return ritual and protect access to it.

Step 5: Recommit in Writing:

At the end of every month, write one page to yourself. What did you choose this month from your born identity? Where did you betray yourself? What do you choose for the month ahead? This practice of regular recommitment is how belonging becomes permanent.

Self-belonging is not selfishness. It is the prerequisite for everything else — your relationships, your service, your impact. You cannot pour from an empty vessel, and you cannot give what you have not first become.

Building Self-Trust When You Don't Know Who You Are Yet

Here is something I've learned about self-trust that we don't hear often. It's hard to trust yourself when you are still in the middle of figuring out who you are. When you have spent years building your identity on something that turned out to be formed rather than born, and you are now in that in-between space of I know who I was and I'm not sure yet who I am — trusting yourself can feel like trying to stand on ground that is still shifting.

But here is something else I learned: you do not have to have it all figured out to start trusting yourself. You just have to start making decisions from your gut rather than your fear.

Fear-based decisions are reactive. Urgent. Driven by what might happen if you don't. Gut-based decisions feel different. More settled. There is a rightness to them, a sense of alignment. Like something in you is nodding "mhmm, that's it."

Not your emotions. Your emotions are real and deserve to be felt, but emotions are not always a reliable compass when you are healing. They can be shaped by old wounds and old fears still running in the background.

Your gut — that deep, instinctive, body-level knowing — is older than your fear. It is closer to your born identity than almost anything else you have access to. Learn to hear it.

What Belonging to Yourself Actually Looks Like

A woman who belongs to herself walks into a room without scanning it for approval. She is not performing for the audience. She is not auditioning for a role. She is simply there…present, herself, enough. She says no and does not spiral into guilt. She says yes and means it fully, freely, without resentment building underneath.

She is not finished. Polished, not perfect. She still has hard days and old patterns that surface without warning. She still catches the performance creeping back in. But she notices. And she comes back.

That is the difference. Not perfection. Return.

A woman who belongs to herself knows how to come back to herself. No matter how far the noise of life pulls her. Because she knows the way home now. And home — as we talked about in the last chapter — is her.

"Trust in the Lord with all your heart and lean not on your own understanding; in all your ways submit to him, and he will make your paths straight." — Proverbs 3:5-6

REFLECT

In what areas of your life have you been looking outside yourself for belonging?

What does self-betrayal feel like in your body before you even fully realize you're doing it?

Who in your life has benefited from your smallness and what would it mean to stop performing for them?

What is one decision you need to make from your gut right now that fear has been talking you out of?

____

____

____

____

CHAPTER NINE

RECLAIM. REBUILD. RADIATE.

To be real is to embrace your authenticity. To be rooted is to know who you are and your worth from the beginning. To be radiant is to shine from it.

You made it.

Not just to the end of this book, to the end of a version of yourself that was never fully yours to begin with.

I want you to sit with that for a moment. Because the fact that you are still here, still willing, still doing the honest and uncomfortable work of looking at yourself clearly, that is not nothing. That is everything.

Reclaim

To reclaim yourself is not to become someone new. It is to become someone original. The woman you are reclaiming was not built in therapy or discovered in a self-help book. She was born. She was there before the wounds, before the labels, before the survival mode, before the formed identity was layered over the real one like coat after coat of paint on a wall that was beautiful to begin with. She is the little girl who wanted to play piano instead of softball. She is the woman who sat at a lagoon in Belize and heard a whisper in the silence that sounded just like her. She is the one who was known — really known — before she was ever formed.

Reclaiming her does not mean pretending the years of forming didn't happen. It does not mean erasing your story or acting as if the survival mode didn't serve you in the seasons when you needed it most.

It means choosing her anyway. Alongside all of it. Through all of it. That is reclamation. Not rejection of your past. Integration of it — with eyes open and a hand extended toward the woman who has been waiting underneath.

Rebuild

Here is what I want you to know about rebuilding. The promise of restoration sounds good, but the process does not always feel good. And there is something important I need you to understand before you begin: rebuilding is not renovation. You are not taking the old structure and upgrading the fixtures. You are not patching the cracks and repainting the walls and calling it transformation. That is not rebuilding. That is maintenance with better lighting.

Rebuilding starts at the foundation. And the only foundation that holds is knowing who you are. Not who you performed. Not who you survived into. Not who the world decided you were before you had a say in the matter. The real work — the hardest work — is dying to an identity you've always known in order to make room for the one that was always true.

To be rooted is to know who you are and to know your worth, not as something you earned, not as something you are still working toward, but as something you were born with. Something that was never contingent on the right circumstances, the right relationships, or the right season. Something no loss could take. No rejection could diminish. No stretch of failure could disqualify you from.

Your worth is not a reward for performance. It is a birthright.

And when you build your life on that — when every decision, every relationship, every yes and every no flows from a woman who knows she is already enough — everything changes.

Not because your circumstances become perfect. Life will still bring loss and transition and seasons that shake you. But the foundation holds. Because it is not built on what you've done or what you've achieved or what people have said about you. It is built on something real. Something true. Something no one gave you and no one can take away.

FRAMEWORK: YOUR RECLAIM. REBUILD. RADIATE. ACTION PLAN

This is your 90-day forward plan. Not a to-do list, a direction. A set of commitments that move you from understanding to living. Complete one section at a time. Revisit every 30 days.

Step 1: RECLAIM: Days 1-30

Choose one thing from your born identity column that you have been neglecting. Schedule it into your week, not as a reward for completing everything else, but as a non-negotiable. Protect it. Show up for it. Tell someone you trust what you're doing and why.

Step 2: REBUILD: Days 31-60

Identify one relationship, habit, or commitment in your life that is built on your formed identity, on performance, fear, or the need to be needed. This month, begin to renegotiate it. You don't have to blow it up. Just begin to shift your participation from obligation to genuine choice.

Step 3: RADIATE: Days 61-90

Choose one space where you will show up fully as your born identity, unapologetically, without shrinking, without performing. A conversation you've been avoiding. A room you've been afraid to take up space in. A gift you've been holding back. This month, you let her show up. All of her.

Step 4: Monthly Review

At the end of each 30-day cycle, write answers to these three questions: Where did I choose my born identity this month? Where did I revert to my formed identity and what triggered it? What do I want to intentionally choose next month?

Step 5: The Ripple Commitment

Before you close this book, write down one woman in your life who needs to read it. Not to fix her. Not to rescue her. But because her story matters and she deserves to come home to herself too. Belonging to yourself makes you safer for others to belong to themselves.

This is not a sprint. It is a lifelong journey. The goal is not to perfect the plan; it is to stay in the direction. Every time you choose your born identity over your formed identity, you are building the life you were made for.

Radiate

And then… this.

When you are real and you are rooted, something happens that you cannot manufacture and you cannot perform your way into.

> *You shine.*

Not the shine of a woman trying to be seen. Not the shine of achievement or applause or the perfectly curated image. The shine of a woman who is so aligned with who she actually is that her presence does something in a room without her trying.

To be radiant is to shine from the inside out.

That is the difference between a woman performing her light and a woman living in it. One is exhausting. The other is effortless. One fades when the audience leaves. The other just keeps going, in the quiet moments and the hard ones and the ordinary Tuesdays when nothing remarkable is happening but something true is.

Live aligned with who you are and the pressure to perform will fade, and the power to impact will rise.

This is what I want for you. Not a bigger platform. Not more applause. Not a more impressive version of the formed identity you've been carrying. Impact. The kind that outlives you.

The kind that doesn't need your name attached to it to keep doing its work in the world. The kind that comes not from how well you performed but from how honestly you lived.

Because here is what I know after everything — after the softball field and the stroke and the lagoon in Belize and the songs written in the middle of the breaking and the long, slow, sacred work of coming home to myself:

> *The pressure to perform fades when you live aligned with who you are.*

What I Want You to Walk Away Knowing

Before you close this book, I want to say a few more things directly to you. Not to the reader. Not to the audience. To you. The one who picked this book up because something in the title felt uncomfortably familiar. The one who recognized herself in the softball story. The one who has been quietly exhausted for longer than she wants to admit.

You are not too far gone.

You are not too broken, too lost, too formed, too complicated, too much, or too far behind. You are simply a woman in the middle of her becoming. And becoming is not a destination you arrive at. It is a direction you choose. Every day. In the small decisions and the quiet moments and the times when the old patterns surface and you must choose — again — who is going to live your life.

Choose her. The real one.

Remember to discover what stirs your soul and let yourself be stirred by it. Let your presence speak louder than your performance. Stop waiting for the applause that was never going to fill you anyway and start building the life that was always meant to be yours. You were not born to perform. You were born to bear fruit.

And the fruit that grows from a woman who is real, who is rooted, who is radiant from the inside out?

> *It outlives her.*

It lives in the women she touched who finally gave themselves permission. In the daughters watching how she moves through the world. In the rooms she walked into fully, without apology, without performance, without shrinking, and left changed simply by being there. That is your legacy.

Not the titles. Not the achievements. Not the perfectly maintained image. *You.*

Real. Rooted. Radiant.

That has always been enough. It always will be.

To be real is to embrace your authenticity.

To be rooted is to know who you are and your worth from the beginning.

To be radiant is to shine from it.

Welcome home.

"The Son is the radiance of God's glory and the exact representation of his being" — Hebrews 1:3

REFLECT

What does reclaiming yourself look like in this specific season of your life?

____

____

____

____

What does it mean to you personally to be real, rooted, and radiant?

____

____

____

____

What is one thing you are ready to stop performing starting today?

____

____

____

____

What fruit do you want your life to bear that outlives you?

____

____

____

____

What would you tell the woman you were at the beginning of this book?

____

____

____

____

ABOUT THE AUTHOR

Tacondra L. Brown is a life-transforming love, an explorer, creative, and lover of all thing's beauty. She's also an author, speaker, and foundational architect who is the founder of MetamorpHERsis and The Whole Woman Grove Community—platforms dedicated to helping women grow in faith, to transform, reclaim their identity, and rebuild their lives from the inside out.

Drawing from her own journey through loss, caregiving, spiritual wrestling, and the slow, holy work of coming home to herself, Tacondra writes and speaks with the kind of honesty that makes women feel less alone and more awake to who they were always made to be. She is a transformational coach, creative entrepreneur, and Counselor in training living in the Central Texas area. She is the proud mother of one daughter and married to her childhood sweetheart, Eric. When she is not writing or working with women, you can find her exploring the world, on a cruise, behind a camera, simply being or creating—fully, singing and playing the music she was born to create.

Connect with Tacondra:

www.tacondra.com